The Mystery Of
Sacred Salmon
— AND —
Native Alaskans

By Randy Persson

Illustrations by Thomas Rodriguez

INKWELL BOOKS
Writing-Publishing-Printing

ISBN: 979-8-9880779-6-1
Library of Congress Control Number: 2020994263

Published by Inkwell Books LLC
10632 North Scottsdale Road, Unit 695
Scottsdale, AZ 85254
Tel. 480-315-3781
E-mail info@inkwellbooksllc.com
Website www.inkwellbooksllc.com

INKWELL BOOKS
Writing-Publishing-Printing

Dedication

I dedicate this book to Rjay Lloyd, my best friend,
his wonderful wife Ann and their adventure loving children,
Amy, Holly, Allison, Mary Ann, and Brian.

Friends are to be treasured and the Lloyd family
is a treasure unlike any I have ever known.

Forward

Drew and I are brothers, my name is Taylor, and we love to travel and solve mysteries of nature.

We took this trip to Alaska with our dad and really didn't know what to expect. And then the adventure began. We flew to Anchorage, got in a small plane piloted by a bush pilot, and flew into a remote area northeast of Anchorage. Then we got on a boat and went upstream to a fishing lodge.

Next came bears and salmon and scary stuff.

The salmon's life cycle and their migration from the river to the ocean and back to the river is amazing.

Also amazing is the history of Native Alaskans whose ancestors migrated across the Bering Land Bridge from Siberia to Alaska.

An incredible adventure and we hope you enjoy following along with us in the vast untamed wilderness that is Alaska.

Contents

CHAPTER 1

North to Alaska

"This is your captain speaking. Fasten your seatbelts. We are cleared to land in Anchorage."

"Anchorage, Alaska," I said out loud. "Wow, we are here!"

My younger brother, Drew, anxiously looked out the airplane window and blurted out, "Look Taylor, an ice-blue ocean and mountain peaks covered with snow! Can this be Alaska? I don't see any totem poles or polar bears?"

Ok, you have to love my brother; he says what's on his mind and sometimes he can be hilarious.

Sitting in the seat next to Drew, Dad said, "Drew, we're at the doorstep of Alaska, and we will see all it has to offer. We may see brown and black bears, moose, eagles, beavers, and many other animals as we learn about the migration of salmon in the rivers and Pacific Ocean. Get ready for a true adventure that includes the mysterious life cycle of the salmon and their symbol of wisdom that dates back 15,000 years to ancient civilizations."

Rjay, Dad's best friend, invited us to join him and his son Brian, on a fishing trip to the Talaview Lodge, in the Alaska wilderness 70 miles northwest of Anchorage. We enjoy fishing and are always looking for another adventure, so we were fortunate Rjay asked us to join them on this trip to the interior of south-central Alaska.

The plane touched down and we grabbed our backpacks from the overhead bin and headed for the exit doors.

We stepped off the plane and the cool clean air tickled my nose.

Rjay said, "Welcome to Alaska." He paused and then with his arms outstretched he continued, "The name Alaska is derived from the *Unangax* (Aleut) word *alaxsxa* or *alaxsixix*, both meaning mainland or great land. Alaska is huge and nearly one-third of the state lies within the Article Circle with most of it underlain by permafrost which is frozen sediment and rock. Ok, enough about the geography of Alaska, let's walk over to baggage claim and pick up our luggage."

We got our luggage off the baggage carousel, walked through the airport, picked up a rental van and drove to the Anchorage Sheraton Hotel where we will stay for the night.

On the way to the hotel, Drew piped up, "Rjay, are we going to see polar bears?"

Rjay and Dad chuckled and Rjay said, "Well Drew, the polar bears are in northern Alaska where they live and hunt seals on ice flows. Here, in the middle of the interior of Alaska, we will fish for salmon, and we may see bears fishing alongside us."

So, I think to myself, we are going to learn about salmon and at the same time fish for them with the bears. What have we gotten ourselves into?

Dad added, "Rjay is a world traveler and loves hunting and fishing. He never tires of another adventure, whether fishing in Alaska or on Safari in Africa. He and Brian will share their experiences with us, and they will be our guides on this adventure into the wild country of Alaska."

After we left the airport and drove into Anchorage, Rjay stopped the van in front of Mossy's Fly shop and said, "We will rent waders here."

"Waders, what are waders?" I asked.

Dad said, "We will be fly fishing for salmon and the best way to catch them is to stand in the middle of the river and cast. To stay dry, we will wear waders, which are rubber overalls that you put on over your clothes. Mike Brown, owner of Mossy's, will fit us for the waders and give us some tips on which flies to use for fishing this time of year."

"Fly fishing," said Drew, "I thought we were fishing for salmon, not flies!"

Dad and Rjay smiled and laughed, and Rjay said, "Ok Drew, there are many ways to catch fish in Alaska. Salmon eat insects and we will be using very long fly rods with artificial flies tied to the end of our fishing lines that look like the insects the salmon eat. When we get to the Lodge, I will teach you and Taylor how to cast a fly rod.

It's not that hard and with a little practice I know you can do it."

Mike said, "Best flies to catch Kings are the chartreuse, blue and green flies."

"Thanks Mike," said Rjay, "great advice. We will take two dozen flies and watch out salmon!"

One last look around the store and I said, "We are a long way from Arizona, and I hope the bears will want to catch salmon and not us for dinner!"

CHAPTER 2

Bush Pilot

We checked into the Sheraton Anchorage Hotel and went up to our rooms. We were too excited to sleep but we tried and finally, exhausted from the day's travels, we fell asleep.

Buzz, Buzz, the alarm went off. I got up, looked outside, and it was overcast with gray clouds. How can it be morning when we just went to sleep? And no sooner than I got back into bed, there was a knock at the door, and I heard Dad say, "Hey sleepyheads, time to get up. See you downstairs in 20 minutes for breakfast."

We went downstairs to the main level, and we saw a beautiful spiral staircase with a waterfall under it. Dad said, "The staircase is made out of jade, and we are going to have breakfast at the Jade Restaurant where you can order reindeer sausage or lox, which is smoked salmon, and an everything bagel with cream cheese."

Ok, this is different. Reindeer sausage or salmon for breakfast! Well, I ordered the reindeer sausage and Dad had the lox and they were both terrific. Great breakfast, if not a little unusual.

After breakfast, we checked out and got into our rented van. Rjay said, "We are going to the Lake Hood Seaplane Base where we will meet Chris and he will introduce us to the bush pilot, who will fly us into the interior of Alaska. Bush pilots are highly trained, experienced pilots known for safely flying smaller airplanes in rugged, or 'bush,' terrain. They provide all kinds of services to remote communities, like an ambulance when necessary and very often face harsh weather conditions. Our pilot is very experienced, and he will fly us to our destination in the 'bush' and since there is no airport or runway where we are going, he will land on the river."

Drew looked concerned and said, "The plane will land on a river? Planes don't land on water! Won't the plane sink in the river with us on it?"

Brian, who loves to fly and has taken this trip before, explained that the plane will have pontoons on it instead of tires. With the pontoons, the plane can land on the water, and it is up to the pilot to pick the best place to land the plane.

"Seriously?" said Drew. "We get into a small plane and fly to a river where the pilot lands on water. I'm not so sure about this!!"

Dad smiled and said, "Drew, there are no roads where we are going and the only way to get to the Lodge is to fly in."

At the Seaplane Base, we saw a red and white plane with giant floats where the tires should be. Dad explained that this plane is part of a fleet of planes in Rust's Air Service and the pilot is a bush pilot who flies people into the remote areas of Alaska without airports or landing strips. And Rjay, who is a pilot himself, said, "This plane is a six-seater fixed-wing de Havilland Beaver equipped with floats so it can land on the water. Now, grab your suitcase and backpack and stow it in the cargo compartment of the plane and let's get ready for takeoff."

We climbed up the side of the plane, lowered our heads in the narrow space and got into our seats right behind the pilot. The pilot handed us headsets and told us to put them on.

Brian explained, "The airplane engine is right in front of us and is very loud and deafening. For us to talk to one another, we will speak through the microphone on the headset."

The pilot started the engine, and it was really loud, so I was glad I had the headset on.

We taxied out into the harbor and the engine got louder and louder as we picked up speed skimming over the top of the water. In an instant, we are thrown back in our seats as the plane lifted off the water into the blue sky.

Once we were above the trees, the plane leveled off and Drew said, "Look, there are ducks over there taking off just like we did, and they don't have headsets!"

"Yes," said Dad, "you can call us ducks today and sit back and enjoy the ride."

We were quiet as we climbed higher into the sky and saw the

land getting smaller as we looked out the windows.

After a long time flying over marshes, meandering rivers and tall trees, the pilot began a descent and slowed the planes airspeed.

Drew, "Are we going to crash?"

"No Drew," said Rjay, "we are nearing the spot in the Talachulitna River where the pilot will land the plane. Watch him maneuver the plane ever so carefully as we approach the river."

The plane rocked back and forth in the wind, and we could only see trees and a sand bar ahead of us. Suddenly, a ribbon of river appeared, and the pilot dipped the nose of the plane down, and with a mighty splash of the pontoons, we landed on the river. "Phew," said Drew, "that was scary, but we made it!"

The pilot taxied the plane upriver to an opening on the riverbank and there stood Steve Johnson, the manager of the Talaview Lodge, waving his hands and smiling—he looked glad to see us. A young man, Matt, was by his side and just behind them were two boats pulled up on the riverbank to take us and our gear farther upriver to the Lodge.

"A boat is next?" I asked.

"Yes," said Rjay, "we will take the boats upriver to the Lodge. The plane can't go any further because the river is shallow and there is no place he can land safely."

We loaded our gear into the boats and headed upriver. The river's current was strong and even though the boats had powerful outboard motors, we could not go very fast as we crossed the rapids and bounced over the waves coming at us.

Finally, Steve and Matt steered the boats into a small cove toward a dock and Steve said, "We are here. Grab your gear and follow me up the hill to the Lodge. Your new home away from home."

Again, I think to myself, what have we gotten ourselves into and at that moment Drew said, "I'm hungry, when are we going to eat?" He is always hungry and that's my little brother.

CHAPTER 3

The Lodge and Bears

We walked up the steep and winding path to the Lodge and on our way, Steve pointed out which cabin was for me and Drew and said that Dad would stay in the double cabin up the hill with Rjay and Brian. Our cabin is an A-frame, with a metal roof and wooden shingles for siding. Steve told us that our cabin had one narrow wooden platform on each side of the door. We are to unroll our sleeping bags on top of the platform and that will be our bed. He said there is one extra blanket for each of us and we may need it because the electricity to the cabin is turned off each night. We learned that the electricity to the cabins is supplied by a generator next to the Lodge and at ten o'clock it is turned off to save fuel. With a cautious and serious look he said that we should be sure to lock the door when we both go into and leave our cabin, so we don't have furry visitors in the night.

The cabin was our nighttime home for now and it was certainly better to be inside than sleep outside with bears and other 'furry visitors!'

We stopped at our cabin, unrolled our sleeping bags on the wooden platforms, and put our backpacks and luggage at the end of the beds. After a quick look around the cabin, we walked up to the Lodge for dinner. Dad, Rjay, and Brian were waiting for us, and we all sat down at a long table with wooden chairs. It has been a long day, and our first meal was appropriately salmon, mashed potatoes, and a juicy and yummy apple cobbler for dessert.

Dinner over, we moved into the large family room with soft leather couches and Rjay said, "Before we call it a night, come over to the

window and see what's on the deck."

As we approached the window, Drew suddenly stood at attention and waved his arms in the air. He seemed unable to speak as he backed up quickly, almost falling, away from the window and yelled, "Bear! It's a big black bear. There's a bear on the deck. Is he going to try to get into the Lodge and have us for dinner?"

Brian calmly walked up to us and said, "Taylor and Drew, the bears will leave us alone, and we have to remember we are guests in their forest, so we don't want to disturb them, especially if there is a female bear with her cubs and she feels threatened."

"No way!" said Drew, "I'm not threatening any bears. I will stay close to all of you."

The bear saw us, looked directly into the Lodge through the large window to the deck and we wondered what's next. Then, he slowly turned and ambled down the path to the river. That was a close call.

We moved away from the window and settled into the couches, a little shaken but alive.

Rjay, sitting in front of us, smiling and relaxing said, "Yes, this is Alaska and, as you can see, there are no city lights up here or fast-food drive-thrus; just wildlife everywhere. As Brian said, this is their home, and we are their guests. Bears, moose and other animals are wild animals, and we always need to be aware of their presence. As long as we stay clear of them and mind our own business, we should be ok."

"Taylor and Drew," said Rjay, "do you want me to walk you to your cabin?"

"Yes, please," both Drew and I said in unison, which got chuckles from everyone.

The sky was silver-gray and the air damp as we reached our cabin. Rjay said good night and reminded us to lock the door.

Just before we locked the door, Drew said, "You know, the bear was probably hungry, and I have some candy in my backpack I can throw out the door before we close it."

"Drew, that may not be a good idea. I don't think we are supposed to feed the bears."

"Oh, what can it hurt, and the bear may like it."

Drew threw out the candy and we quickly closed and locked the door.

We crawled into our sleeping bags and still unnerved by seeing the bear on the deck, we talked about this and that with no real subject—just nervous chatter.

After about an hour when we finally calmed down, we heard sounds like someone or something trying to open the door.

"Taylor, what's that?"

"I don't know but it doesn't sound good. Go look out the window and see what it is."

"No," said Drew, "you go—you're older and bigger."

I slowly pulled back my sleeping bag and carefully and quietly walked to the window.

When I reached the window, the window was fogged up, so I wiped off the moisture with my sleeve, and there, looking back at me, was a bear even bigger than the one we saw on the deck. Did I scream, absolutely, and I jumped back into my bed, covered my head with the sleeping bag only to have Drew jump in with me and we both laid there shivering and scared out of our minds.

More pawing and grunting at the door and we were convinced this was the end since we were trapped in the cabin with no cell phones to call for help, no back door, and no escape.

In what seemed like an eternity with me and Drew clinging to each other and hearing footsteps and grunting outside our cabin, it got eerily silent and all we could hear was the wind in the trees.

"Drew," I said, "maybe the bear has given up and gone away. I don't think tossing candy to the bears is a good idea. Now get back in your own sleeping bag and no more feeding the bears or we could be their midnight snack."

CHAPTER 4

The Sacred Salmon

We didn't sleep well and woke up to a loud pounding at our door. I whispered to Drew, "Oh no, the bear is back and wants to get in."

Then we heard a familiar voice, "Taylor, Drew, it's Dad. Time to get up!"

"Dad, thank goodness it's you and not that bear. Give us a minute. It's cold in our cabin and we had a scary night; can we sleep a little longer please?"

I heard Dad laugh and say, "The salmon are waiting for us so get a move on!!"

We dressed and made our way to the Lodge in the grey morning mist. Rjay, Dad and Brian were waiting for us with huge smiles. We are just a couple of bleary-eyed city boys out in the woods scared to death we are going to be eaten by bears. But we know adventure awaits so we need to pull ourselves together.

Steve and Louise set out a delicious pancake breakfast with warm maple syrup and Rjay said, "While you are waking up and eating your breakfast, I want to tell you about the amazing salmon.

The Pacific salmon have been around as far back as 4 to 6 million years. Salmon bones were found at an Alaskan settlement that dates back 11,500 years showing the fish was an important food source for the tribes in the region.

The salmon was known to the ancient Sumerian and Babylonian cultures and has been revered and considered sacred for over 20,000 years. The fish was recognized by early indigenous communities and its sanctity was revered by Buddhism, Hinduism and Christianity, whose earliest icon was a fish."

"Whoa," said Drew, "that's amazing. And these salmon in Alaska are the same fish that were around 20,000 years ago?"

"Yes Drew," continued Rjay, "and during this trip we will delve deeper into the salmon's extraordinary journey and amazing lifecycle which begins and ends in rivers. They are hatched in spawning grounds, then swim in the river for about a year as they make their way down to the Pacific Ocean. Once they reach the ocean, they spend the next 2 to 3 years growing big and strong before they begin the long journey back to their birthplace in the same river where their life began."

Drew said, "And then what do they do? They must be exhausted after swimming all the way from the ocean up the river against the current."

"Yes, Drew, you are correct. They stop eating when they leave the ocean and begin their journey home in the river. The distances they must swim and the waterfalls they must jump over is so very hard on them that once they reach the spawning grounds and fertilize the eggs, they die from weakness. You may say they sacrifice themselves so the next generation may live."

"Wait a minute," said Drew, "this is a sacred fish that returns to where it was born only to die?"

"It is a heroic fish Drew and its life's journey to and from the ocean is a mystery of nature. I ask you, how could salmon travel down a river and out to the ocean covering up to 8,000 miles only to return to the exact spot where they were born?"

We all sat silently thinking about this beautiful fish, its history, amazing journey, and lifecycle.

"Ok," said Rjay, "here's a little more information about the salmon.

You probably know that the rivers are fresh water, the ocean is saltwater, and most fish cannot live in both. The salmon, however, can live in both as evidenced by the fact they were born in a freshwater river and then live many years in the saltwater ocean. They are unique in that they can travel between fresh and saltwater and thrive in each. Their mastery of the two realms was one of the reasons ancient cultures regarded the salmon as wise. The word 'salmon' comes from the Latin, salire, meaning 'to leap', which is what may have drawn attention to the fish in the first place. Leaping up waterfalls aside, the salmon is most known for its ability to return to its birthplace after many years to give birth to a new generation and then, as you will see, to die. Their destiny is to travel vast distances upstream, and along the way they have to not only defy gravity by scaling waterfalls but also evade a variety of predators such as bears, beavers, birds of prey and humans—all who want to catch them and feast on their succulent and nourishing body."

"Rjay," I asked, "are we going to catch and eat these heroic and wonderful salmon?"

"Yes and no. We are sportsmen and we are going to fish with barbless hooks so we can catch and release most of the salmon without hurting them. We will keep some salmon for Louise to cook for us while we are here, and we will pack some in dry ice and take them back to Arizona to enjoy with our families and friends."

"Catch and release. What's that?" Drew asked. "The bears don't catch and release, do they?"

"The salmon provides a needed and nutritious food source for the bears so no; they don't release them. The bears and other predators rely on the salmon as a valuable food source to get them through the long cold winter."

Drew asked, "Are there different types of salmon, or are they all alike?"

"Good question Drew," said Brian, "there are five types of wild Alaskan salmon, Chinook, Sockeye, Coho, Chum and Pink. Each species returns from the ocean to their spawning grounds at different times of the summer. We are here in June when the type of salmon returning to its home is the King Salmon, the biggest salmon."

Brian continued; "The Chinook Salmon, otherwise known as King Salmon, is the state fish of Alaska. They earned the royal name because these fish are the largest species of salmon. They can weigh up to 125 pounds. King Salmon represent authority, power, grandeur, and leadership.

The other salmon are the Chum Salmon which are known for their adventuresome spirits; Coho Salmon, which have the nickname of Silvers because of the color of their skin and are known for their psychic awareness and vision; the Pink Salmon, the smallest of the species and their skin color is pink and they are known for their playfulness friendship and romance; and the last species is the Sockeye Salmon, and they are the most colorful of all and are called Reds and their variety of colors represents diversity.

In the Talachulitna River, the King Salmon run from late June through mid-July. The Sockeye Salmon run from Late July through mid-August and the Silvers run the entire month of August.

So, the river is plentiful with three different types of salmon most of the summer."

Brian added, "Let's finish breakfast, get our fishing rods and head down to the river and see if we can find the mighty salmon on their journey upstream to their spawning grounds."

CHAPTER 5

The Kings Return

With salmon swimming in our heads, we finally began our day. We walked out onto the deck of the Lodge, put on our waders, grabbed our fly rods, and walked down to the dock where Steve and Matt were waiting for us by the boats.

Steve and Louise live at the Lodge year-round, and Steve knows where and when the salmon swim upstream to their spawning grounds. Matt is a new guide and is learning the business from Steve.

At the boats, Steve said, "Your trip timing is excellent. The Kings are running, and we will take the boats down to where the Skwentna River meets the Talachulitna River, and I believe there will be great fishing there."

We packed the rods, fishing tackle boxes and other equipment in the boat captained by Matt and we all got into the second boat captained by Steve.

We pushed off from the riverbank, Steve and Matt started the motors and we headed downstream.

Drew said, "It's cold on the water. Will it warm up when we start fishing?"

Rjay said, "Believe me, once we start fishing and you catch a big King, the weather will be the farthest thing from your mind."

We rounded a corner and ran into the branches of a tree that had fallen into the river. We quickly ducked down to the bottom of the boat hoping we could pass under it. "Rjay," Steve yelled, "look out!"

Sure enough, the boat got caught under the tree and we lost Rjay because he couldn't get to the bottom of the boat—there wasn't enough room for him.

"Dad," I yelled, "where's Rjay?"

Lying with our heads down on the bottom of the boat, we finally felt the current move the boat ever so slightly, and as we passed under a low hanging branch, we heard a thump at the back of the boat. A bear I wondered.

"Wait, it's Rjay." Steve said, "We didn't know what happened to you. Are you ok?"

Rjay smiled, brushed off the pine needles from his coat and said, "When I realized there was no room in the boat for me under the tree branches, I decided to jump out of the boat and climb up on one of the tree limbs. When I saw the boat slowly pass under the limb, I jumped back into the boat and here I am!"

"Rjay," Steve said, "after all these years fishing with you, you never cease to amaze me. You think quickly and you climb trees better than bears!"

We all laughed and were grateful Rjay was back in the boat safe and sound.

Steve said, "There are no more trees in the river, and you can see just ahead of us, the junction of the two rivers. That's where we will stop on the sand bar between the rivers and start fishing." Steve steered the boats onto a sand bar, we got out and pulled them up on the sand leaving only the back of the boats and motors in the water.

Drew said pointing, "Look, look over there." Sure enough,

there was a huge moose on the far side of the river walking slowly along the bank. Steve said, "Let's all be quiet while we get our rods out, so we don't disturb the moose. This is his home and I'm sure he is as curious about us as we are about him."

We got our rods, Steve showed us how to tie on the special fly we bought at Mossey's and said, "Wade into the river and cast toward the rapids—that's where the fish will be."

I was enjoying the quiet, the cool moist air, water tugging at my waders, the blue sky and then Drew yelled, "AEEE, something took my hook."

Rjay, standing in the river just to the right of Drew said, "You've hooked a salmon, raise the tip of your rod and begin to reel him in."

Drew looked petrified as he tried to follow Rjay's instructions and suddenly, the biggest fish I have ever seen jumped six feet out of the water turning sideways before diving back into the water.

"Now what, Rjay?" said Drew. Rjay said, "You are in for a fight. Stay calm and keep the line between you and that monster fish as tight as possible."

Almost at the same time, each of us had a fish on our line and Drew was on his own.

All of us with fish on our lines looked like a fire drill running up and down the river, trying not to lose the fish and at the same time trying not to cross each other's line. Yup, I thought, this is just like clowns with baggy pants and floppy shoes running around each other at the circus, trying not to fall over one another.

My heart was pounding, my feet slipping on the rocky bottom of the river, and the fish jumping like it was an Olympic sport. I honestly thought I was in a different universe.

CHAPTER 6

Fishing For Kings

In all the commotion that was surrounding us trying to catch our fish Rjay, by far the best fisherman, was about to land the first fish. Steve quietly stepped towards Rjay's line and gently placed a large net around the huge, beautiful bright red fish. We all watched as Steve expertly took the fish out of the water and held it up so we could all see it.

"Wow," said Drew, "that's huge!" With his attention now on Rjay's fish, Drew's fish took off upstream and pulled on Drew's line so hard that Drew stumbled, let go of the line, and the fish turned and threw the hook out of his mouth.

"Drew," said Dad, "get yourself together, bring in your line and I'll bet there is another fish out there waiting for you to match its strength against yours. Never forget that the Kings are big strong fish and have lived in the rivers and the ocean avoiding prey and getting stronger every day. And they are smart or as we are told by many, they are wise."

We spent the morning catching more fish and the hours seemed to fly by when Steve said, "Ok, everyone, time for lunch."

At that moment when we stopped fishing, I felt my arms and legs aching. Fishing is fun, but it is tiring, especially when you are catching huge fish using a lightweight fly rod. Breaking for lunch and resting were good ideas.

Louise had packed lunch for us, and we sat on the sand bar and ate our sandwiches.

Rjay said, "As soon as lunch is over, we are going to another spot upriver where there are more Kings, and we may see a bear or two because there are rapids where we are going, and the bears like to fish there."

Drew looked concerned and said, "Bears? We are going to fish with bears. I've seen enough bears for one trip. What if we look like a better lunch for them than the fish?"

We all laughed out loud. Dad, with a big smile said, "Yes Drew, you will have to keep your eyes open and please don't cast your line in the direction of a bear. Who knows, you may catch one and then what will you do?"

Lunch over, we leaned back on the sand and rested for about a half hour and then packed our rods and gear into the boats and headed to what Steve called "Bear Flats."

Going upstream was a lot slower than going downstream, so it took almost an hour to get to Bear Flats. We were nervous about fishing with bears and the whole time we hoped they would prefer fish to us for lunch.

Finally, we saw the rapids and no bears. "Where are the bears?" asked Drew. "Is this Bear Flats?"

Steve said, "Maybe the bears are napping after morning fishing. Let's beach our boats on the other side of the river and start fishing. If the bears come down to the river, they like walking in the rapids to look for fish and we will stand in the middle of the river and cast away from the rapids."

At this point, we knew what to do, so we got out of the boat, walked into the river, and took up positions about 20 feet from one another and began to cast.

Wham! Brian caught the first fish, and it was a real fighter. His rod bent over with the tip almost touching the water in a vast arc.

Brian yelled, "Got a big one on my line! Everyone stay clear because this is going to be a tough one to land."

We pulled in our lines to let Brian move up and down the river without getting tangled up in our lines and for more than a half hour, Brian had his hands full.

"Get the net," said Brian, "he's close enough and tired enough I think we can net him."

Rjay grabbed the net and carefully made his way to the end of Brian's line and gently netted the biggest and reddest King Salmon we had seen all day.

"Grab the camera," said Dad, "let's get a photo of the fish before Brian releases him back into the river."

Rjay guessed the salmon weighed well over 45 pounds and it was a beautiful fish.

Just then, two bears appeared on the other side of the river and looked at us like they wanted Brian's fish.

"Hurry," said Rjay, "take the photo and let him go."

Oh my, this is an adventure I will never forget as we let the fish go and backed up toward the riverbank as we watched the two bears take positions in the rapids and begin fishing themselves.

Bears can catch the salmon in their mouths as they jump in the rapids or grab them with their huge claws if they can get one in shallow water.

Fishing was good for the bears, and it didn't take them long to each get a fish, walk back to their side of the river, and eat their salmon lunch right there in front of us.

We watched them eat the fish, which was interesting because they ate the whole fish, and we could hear them loudly crunching the head and bones. When they were done and with parts of the fish all over their faces and paws, they slowly waddled with full stomachs up the riverbank and into the forest.

Rjay said, "You know who else fishes nearby? Beavers! Look over there beyond the rapids and you can see what looks like a brush pile with logs and branches. That's a beaver dam and behind it there is a shallow pool of water where the beavers catch fish.

And look in the sky, an eagle is flying high looking for a meal."

Drew said, "We are fishing with bears, beavers and eagles, what's next, aliens landing on the sand bar and fishing with lasers?"

Like I always say, Drew's mind is busy.

"Ok, everyone," said Rjay, "just animals and no aliens. Today's entertainment is over let's get back to fishing."

We fished for another couple of hours and had a super time catching the Kings. It was late afternoon, and both thrilled and exhausted, we loaded up our rods and gear and headed upstream to the Lodge.

Rjay said, "A great day of fishing for us and the bears. We will all sleep well tonight."

CHAPTER 7

Bering Land Bridge and Native Alaskans

The sky began to turn a dark grey as we approached the dock. We tied up the boats to the dock and, with aching legs and arms, we walked up the long narrow path to our cabins.

Dad said, "Unload your gear in your cabin and head up to the Lodge for dinner."

Once more, Louise had prepared a wonderful dinner of pork chops (flown in from Anchorage), green beans, carrots, and corn from her garden. We sometimes get organic vegetables at home and these fresh garden vegetables picked today are the best I have ever tasted!

After dinner, we went into the family room, got comfortable on the couches and Rjay said, "We have had a wonderful day of fishing and so far, you have seen moose, bears, beavers, and eagles. You have learned that we are in a wilderness and to survive here, like the wild animals, we need food like nutritious salmon and shelter. Think about the first people who came to this area, and they had to find food and shelter. How did they get here and who are they?"

Rjay settled back on the couch and said, "The Indigenous People of Alaska, who are jointly called Native Alaskans, have a rich heritage being the first people to live in Alaska and can be divided into five major groupings: Aleuts, Northern Eskimos (Inupiat), Southern Eskimos (Yuit), Interior Indians (Athabascans) and Southeast Coastal Indians (Tlingit and Haida). We are in an area settled by the Athabaskans. They were accomplished hunters and followed herds of caribou and moose for long distances, fished for salmon and other river fish, and gathered roots, berries, and edible plants."

Drew was curious and asked, "We have Native Americans in Arizona. Are they related to the Native Alaskans?"

"Really good question Drew. The Athabaskans are close relatives of the Navajos and Apaches. In Arizona there are 22 tribes of Native Americans many of whom may be descendants of the tribes that migrated to Alaska from Asia and Siberia starting 11,000 years ago during the last Ice Age. At that time, the glaciers had become larger and larger as they turned water into ice. "

Drew asked, "Migrating tribes and glaciers that turn water into ice. That sounds like a miracle of nature."

"Nature is amazing and so are the glaciers. When water in the ocean evaporates into the atmosphere, it loses its salt content and then returns to earth as snow and rain. Toward the end of the Ice Age, in the northern regions of the earth, it was so cold that glaciers began to form when the snow piled up and the rain and snow froze. The loss of the ocean water through evaporation and rain and snow freezing and getting locked up in glaciers, caused the sea levels to drop. In some areas, it dropped up to 300 feet. The land under the Bering Strait became exposed and a flat grassy treeless plain emerged connecting Asia to North America. This massive expanse was called Beringia and is known as the Bering Land Bridge. This newly dry land exposed by the receding ocean water was pivotal in allowing generations of people migrating from Asia and Siberia to reach Alaska as they chased the animals they hunted for food."

Rjay continued, "As the Ice Age ended and the earth began to warm, glaciers melted, the sea level rose and Beringia became sub-merged once again except for a couple of islands that still poke out of the water between Alaska and Russia."

Rjay gave us a few minutes to let us imagine in our minds the many tribes walking across the vast treeless Bering Land Bridge to Alaska. I can't imagine how difficult that would have been!

Rjay continued, "Tribes have migrated to Alaska principally from Siberia and northern Asia for over 15,000 years, and some believe the earliest tribes came to Alaska during the Stone Age. Those ancient peoples moved with the seasons and followed the animals they hunted. Archaeologists have unearthed spears and other stone tools and have concluded that many different tribes migrated to Alaska over the years, with the largest group crossing from Siberia to Alaska over the Bering Land Bridge.

Those early ancient ones and the following migrating tribes have left signs of their journey and villages all over Alaska. Today, the Native Alaskans living in Alaska are descendants of those tribes. We believe that some migrating tribes settled in Alaska, and others continued moving south to Canada, the United States and even to Central and South America. Researchers believe that certain tribes walked across the Bering Land Bridge while other tribes which were more adapted to the sea, may have crossed the ocean in boats after the ice melted, and made their way down the west coast of Alaska and Canada. All Native Alaskans have a rich history of migration and of sustaining themselves in the wild country."

Drew asked, "What type of animals were the hunters following?"

Brian said, "Bones recovered from the permafrost in Northern Alaska give us a clue as to the types of animals. The hunters chased steppe bison, woolly mammoths, and other large animals."

"And did they fish for salmon?" I asked.

Dad said, "Yes, they were excellent fishers and the salmon in the ocean and rivers were a nutritious food source for them."

"Amazing," I said, "and the descendants of the tribes and the salmon are here today. This is an incredible story of how life continues from generation to generation!"

Rjay leaned forward on the couch and said, "Life is amazing, the Native Alaskans are fantastic, and you will see the final chapter of the life and death journey of the salmon tomorrow when we go upriver to where their life began.

Until tomorrow, good night and now we can appreciate the short migration route to our cozy cabins!"

We all said good night and went to our cabins for one last night in the wilderness and, alas, one more bear encounter.

CHAPTER 8

Salmon's Life Cyle

R ap, rap, rap, "Rise and Shine boys," said a voice at our door. Sleepy and tired, we mustered our strength, got dressed and walked up to the Lodge for breakfast.

"Good morning boys," said Steve, "good to see you made it thru the night without being eaten by a bear." Dad and Rjay chuckled.

"Yes," I said, "we did have a visitor pawing and snorting at our door last night. Probably the same bear, but we weren't about to look for him through the window. We were a little scared with all the noise he was making but our door was locked, and we had a plan to shoo him away."

Dad looked concerned and said, "So what did you do?"

I sat up straight in my chair and said, "We took the bear spray you gave us and shot it at the door hoping that may stop him but the only thing it did was stink up the cabin.

Then we made a lot of noise, and we thought the bear finally got a whiff of the bear spray and with our yelling and screaming and no one tossing food to him, he went away. Thank you, Drew!!"

Rjay said, "Lesson learned. Never feed the bears. They are per-petually hungry and always searching for food—roots, fish, honey, and anything else they can find. Glad you are safe."

"Speaking of food and hunger," Rjay continued, "today we are going to take one boat upstream to where the salmon are heading to spawn."

"Spawn," says Drew, "what's that?"

Rjay says, "You have seen the salmon swimming upstream, and they are heading home. Home to where they were born in this river. When they get to the part of the river where they were born, the female salmon lays hundreds of eggs and the male salmon fertilizes them."

And Brian said, "And then they die right there in the stream."

"Wait," I said, "they are born in the river, swim to the ocean, spend a couple of years in the ocean only to return to where they were born and die? That makes no sense; how do they even know where they were born to begin and end their lives?"

Rjay said, "And that is the mystery of the salmon. Rather than continue to talk about it, let's get in a boat and head upstream."

We finished breakfast thinking about the salmon's travels, walked down the hill to the boat and headed upstream not knowing what to expect.

After about an hour of fighting the current, Steve guided our boat to a sandy riverbank.

Steve said, "Everyone out of the boat and let's climb up this embankment."

We climbed up the riverbank into the forest and we soon came to the edge of a cliff overlooking the river and we saw nothing but bright red in the river.

"Steve," I said, "the river is all red, what is going on?"

Rjay said, "What you are seeing is the hundreds of King Salmon all bunched together at the end of their swim home. It is here where their life began and will end."

Drew asked, "We flew to Anchorage, then flew in a small plane to the Lodge and then took a boat to where we are today. We had maps, GPS, and transportation. How in the world do the salmon know where to go and when?"

"Again, as we talked earlier," Steve said, "that's the mystery of the salmon."

Drew said, "The salmon must have an internal navigation system that tells them where to go. Otherwise, they still would be lost in the ocean."

Rjay said, "Drew, that is a great answer, and it is thought the salmon have an internal navigation system based upon many factors, including the use of magnetic fields that give them the ability to find their way back to the river and spawning grounds where they were hatched. The salmon also have a keen sense of smell and when they are in the ocean and swim by the river that brought them to the ocean, the river has a unique smell, and they know it's time to return to the spawning grounds."

Watching hundreds of bright red salmon below us fertilize eggs and slip back into the current was a life and death scene none of us will ever forget. We could watch all day, but Steve said it's the end of the day and time to leave. We got up and reluctantly got in the boat and headed back to the Lodge. We were noticeably quiet, having witnessed the life-giving mission of the salmon returning to the spawning grounds only to die. They completed this incredible life and death journey by giving all they had to spawn the next generation of mighty salmon.

At the Lodge, we had our last dinner and sat around afterwords talking about all our experiences since we arrived in Alaska.

Drew said, "How can we possibly go home and not remember this life experience. The salmon, the moose, the bears and the land we walked on thousands of years after it was discovered by courageous Native Alaskans. Who would believe us and say we are telling tall tales."

Rjay said, "The experience is ours and it is up to us to pass on the knowledge we have gained to others who may not have the same opportunity we have had. This is real life and not a television show or a video game. Hopefully, when you tell others of our experiences and what we have seen, they will be encouraged to go outside of their homes to take a trip or visit a national park and open their minds to the mysteries of nature. And, perhaps the story of the life cycle of the salmon will give your friends something to consider as they take their own journey on our earth."

Rjay paused to give us time to reflect and said with a knowing smile, "Time to turn in boys, tomorrow we fly out of the wilderness and back to civilization."

We walked quietly back to the cabin, thinking about what Rjay had just said and it was a lot to take in as we reached the cabin.

"Good night, Drew," I said, and Drew said, "Good night, Taylor, what a day. What an adventure."

CHAPTER 9

The Anchorage Museum, Dena'Ina Etnena

We woke up early, got dressed, and Louise fixed us one last special breakfast. She served trout benedict with hollandaise sauce and home fries, and it was delicious. Never did I think I would have trout for breakfast, but this is Alaska, and you eat what you catch.

We thanked Louise for everything, gave her big hugs, grabbed our gear, and got into the boats to meet the pilot downstream.

On our way down the river, Drew saw an eagle, "Look, everyone," he said, "a bald eagle with white head and tail feathers."

Rjay said, "Look what he has in his talons! That salmon he caught was breakfast for him and his family. No Louise to cook it so they will eat it raw just like the bears.

When we get to Anchorage, we are going to the Anchorage Museum. At the museum, you will see the history of the Native Alaskans, a display showing the life cycle of salmon and many exhibits about the animals of Alaska. And Drew, you may finally get to see a totem pole and a polar bear!"

"Really," said Drew, "a totem pole AND a polar bear? I was hoping to see Eskimos too but now I know they don't live in the south of Alaska, so I'll at least get to see a totem pole and a polar bear at the museum."

The pilot landed on the river and taxied to the sand bar. We stowed our gear, got on the plane, and waved goodbye to Steve and Matt. Once again, we were skimming the water like ducks on takeoff and finally the plane lifted us into the air.

We arrived at Anchorage harbor, got in a car Rjay had waiting for us and drove a short distance to the Anchorage Museum.

When we got to the museum Rjay said, "Taylor, Drew, I have a surprise for you." Just then, two men and three boys walked toward us as we entered the museum.

Rjay said, "May I introduce Darin Reber, his two oldest sons, Mitch and Tanner, and Rex Maughan, and his son Gregg. We all work together at Forever Living Products and they are on their way to the Lodge with a short stop at the museum to say hello to us."

Darin said he is very excited to see the museum and couldn't wait to walk around.

We walked together into the museum and realized it was much bigger than expected. Maybe that's because Alaska is bigger than most people think it is.

Drew yelled, "A totem pole! It's huge."

In the large Atrium, there stood a beautiful tall totem pole. We walked over to it and the sign on the base of the pole said that it is the famous Raven-Shark Pole. The pole is 29 feet tall, and the base of the pole is a bear. Above the bear is a downward facing wolf and above the wolf's tail is a shark with small red round nostrils. The fish is long and black and has two dorsal fins and a tail fin. On top is a raven, which is black with red lips on its beak.

Brian, who has done some research on totem poles said, "Totem poles may convey ancestry or history of a particular clan, folklore or real-life experiences or commemorate a person of importance. This pole was once associated as a clan emblem for the Kaagwaantaan clan and today it is used by the Wooshketaan clan. Some totem poles have salmon carvings showing the connection between salmon as a resource that has nourished communities physically and spiritually for thousands of years."

Dad said, "The continuity of the ancient life cycles of the Native Alaskans and the salmon is something we owe to the past, present and future—not unlike our own life cycles."

We continued walking and saw the Discovery Center, the Planetarium, a map showing the early tribes walking across the Bering Land Bridge, the Smithsonian Arctic Studies Center, and many amazing artifacts. We were almost through the museum when we went up the stairs to the Art of the North Galleries. As we entered the gallery, we were surprised to see a feathered hot pink, life-size polar bear, created by the Anchorage-based artist, Paola Pivi.

Drew said, "Finally, a polar bear, a pink polar bear, but still, a polar bear. Taylor, take my picture please so I can show all my friends back home how brave I am. Maybe I'll tell my friends it was a real polar bear that turned pink because it ate too many salmon!"

At that, we all groaned and laughed out loud.

The tour was over and full of Alaskan history and wilderness mysteries, we left the museum and wished our friends a good fishing trip at the Lodge.

Drew, never to be denied, said, "Watch out for the bears and don't feed them candy."

Rex, a seasoned traveler to Alaska who obviously knew not to feed the bears, smiled, looked at Drew and kindly and gently said, "Thank you Drew, great advice."

We got a cab to Anchorage Airport, our last stop, as the sun began to set over the blue water bay.

We returned to our lives in Arizona full of wonderful Alaskan memories. We saw the mysterious life cycle of the salmon, learned about Native Alaskans and most of all—we survived the bears hoping to dine on us at our cabin!

www.ingramcontent.com/pod-product-compliance
Lightning Source LLC
Chambersburg PA
CBHW040855100426

42813CB00015B/2809